What Difference Does It Make?

How the Sexes Differ and What You Can Do About It

Adam Khan
with Klassy Evans

TABLE OF CONTENTS

INTRODUCTION

Women and men are different. Not only do we look different, but we act differently and feel differently. This is not a new revelation. But for the last 40 years the differences between the sexes has been attributed to *social learning*. According to this theory, we really don't have any sexual identity when we're born. A child is *taught* what it means to be female or male, and what we consider feminine behavior or masculine behavior depends on the *culture*.

If a girl was taught that it's feminine to play with toy guns and do a lot of wrestling, she would, and she'd enjoy it just as much as boys do. The theory says that the differences between the sexes are caused by socialization — by what we learned from parents, teachers, television, and our peers.

The theory says we *learned* what is feminine or masculine, and that's why women and men tend to behave and feel differently.

As a matter of fact, the socialization theory is so widespread, for many people it isn't "a theory" at all, it's a self-evident truth.

But lately, this "truth" is being shaken by some very solid research from the fields of biology, genetics, neurology and endocrinology. Scientists all over the world are accumulating research data indicating that many of the differences between the sexes are biological and inborn, and some are not much affected by learning.

That's not to say socialization has no influence. The ability to become socialized — the ability and desire to learn from our own culture — is *itself* a genetically-inherited trait, and a powerful one at that.

Obviously socialization has an influence. But apparently there are some things out of reach of social learning — some feminine or masculine behavior that cannot be unlearned or overridden.

Who Cares?

You might legitimately ask, "What difference does it make? We can see the sexes are different; who cares what the exact *cause* of it is?"

That's a good question. Political issues aside, the answer is: It'll make a difference to you in your relationship with your mate. The differences between the sexes are often a cause of conflict or an underlying source of conflict between a man and a woman.

Most of us *believe* these differences are learned. And of course, if your mate learned it, your mate can (damn well) unlearn it! Right?

But if some of those differences were produced by your mate's biology, and you were convinced no amount of effort could change it, guess what? You'd find it easier to accept your mate for what she or he is, and that would have a *significant* impact on the quality of your relationship.

You may still dislike some of your mate's characteristics, but you would stop frustrating yourself with unfulfilled expectations. And you would learn to work around them.

Look at it this way: If your mate was near-sighted, and you thought nearsightedness was a *learned* condition, it might become a point of friction in your relationship. Maybe you're always on your mate's back when s/he is driving, for example, because it seems to you s/he is "just not paying attention."

If you then discovered that the nearsightedness was something your mate was *born* with and that there wasn't anything s/he can learn to make it better, here's what would happen: 1) your expectations would become more realistic (more fitting given the reality), 2) you would be less frustrated, 3) you'd become more forgiving and understanding, 4) you would have less animosity toward your mate, 5) you would start thinking of ways the two of you could work around your situation rather than simply railing against it (maybe buy some spectacles, for example, or you could do more of the driving). Your relationship would be a happier one.

That's what I want to accomplish with this book: I hope to share enough of the enormous amount of research on this subject that your expectations of your mate become more realistic. With more realistic expectations, you can realistically expect to be more satisfied with your mate. Some of the conflict will disappear from your relationship, and you will find new ways of appreciating each other.

As long as you hold out hope that someday your mate will change, you will be frustrated and disappointed. But if you accept that some differences are irreversible (short of surgery or hormone supplementation) you can begin to work with the *reality* of the situation instead of banging your head against a wall trying to apply the Strictly-Socialization Theory — a theory whose time has come and gone.

IN THE BEGINNING

It all begins at conception. The individual sperm cell that enters the egg determines the sex of the fetus. Female sperm carry more information (the information required for the complex processes of pregnancy and birth) and are therefore heavier than sperm carrying male chromosomes.

Because it is heavier, a sperm carrying female genes moves slower than a sperm carrying male genes. So sperm carrying male genes get there quicker and are more likely to conceive. 125 boys are conceived for every 100 girls.

This difference, right out of the chute, so to speak, is of course *not* the result of socialization.

After conception, females mature faster and are born with a 4 to 6 week developmental head-start over males. This has nothing to do with learning or socialization, either. It is a genetic difference.

About one or two months after conception, if the fetus has an XX chromosome, it begins to produce large amounts of estrogen. If the fetus has an XY chromosome, it begins to produce large amounts of testosterone. These hormones organize the development of not only the body, but also the brain.

Later, the hormone levels go way down, but then increase again at puberty, and remain high into adulthood, activating specific "receptor sites" in the brain and body.

A receptor site in a cell is like a button. The only thing that'll push that button is a specific hormone. For example, there is a molecule very much like testosterone (human male hormone) circulating in the blood of male apes, male birds, male crabs, male fish — just about every male on the planet — and this molecule activates certain behaviors in these animals: strutting, defending territory, displaying plumage, etc.

There are parts of the animal's brain responsible for each of those behaviors. There are receptor sites in those parts of the brain, activated by the male hormone. All of those male-only behaviors are activated by the same hormone.

For example, among certain kinds of song-birds, the male sings but the female does not sing. Inject the female with testosterone, however, and she begins to sing. The receptor sites in the brain are only activated, in this case, by the male hormone. She has the brain circuits installed but they are usually dormant.

If you castrate a male Japanese quail, it will stop copulating and crowing. By castration, you have stopped the production of male hormones. All those receptor sites stop being activated. Give him an injection of male hormone, and he's back to crowing and copulating.

Male fiddler crabs normally have one huge claw and one that's normal size. But castrate a male crab while he is young, and his claws are both normal size as an adult, just like a female.

Back near the beginning of the evolution of animals, DNA divided itself into two sexes, and the development of the male and female sex organs were triggered by a testosterone-like molecule and an estrogen-like molecule.

It's a good adaptation. It's a clean way to create the necessary differences in the sexes. Over time, more and more adaptations were added to each sex.

The two sexes of a single species could now evolve differently, because any adaptation could be triggered only by the male or female hormone.

So if it produced more offspring to have a wider pelvis in the female, the adaptation could be added and triggered *only* by estrogen. And if it wasn't adaptable for males, they could stay as they were.

Human males don't have claws and they don't crow. They may strut a little, but not much. They *do* have testosterone, and women *do* have estrogen, however. As a fetus, the blood levels of these hormones are up to four times the level they will be in childhood. Why? Because there are basic biological differences being hardwired during the fetus's development, making the sexes fundamentally and unalterably different for the rest of their lives.

THE HUMAN SPECIES

In people, these differences show up in hundreds of different ways. For example, June Reinisch, a developmental psychologist, studied 4,653 infants and found that girls sat up without support earlier than boys, and boys crawl earlier than girls, but then crawl for a longer period of time before they learn to walk. The brains of boys also mature more slowly, especially the frontal lobes (responsible, in part, for handling cognitive and social functions).

Keep in mind that these are all *averages*. Individuals vary. But generalizations can be made and they will be true for most people. You can easily say, without argument from most people, that men are taller than women and that women have less body hair than men. Now of course, there are some women who are taller than some men, and there are some men who have less body hair than some women, but by and large, the differences hold true.

In other words, the generalization is very likely true in your relationship.

It is also generally true that women have better nighttime vision, more flexible joints, and a better oxygen supply to the brain. A woman's skin bruises more easily than a man's, and her sweat glands and fat cells are more evenly distributed. She tends to perspire more heavily under her arms, while he perspires more heavily on his chest.

Men have thicker skin, fewer nerve endings on the surface of the skin, a thicker skull, a more slanted forehead and heavier brow ridges (to support larger jaw muscles). Men have tighter joints, better daytime vision and more acute depth perception.

Of course, none of these differences are the result of socialization.

Women have one million fewer red blood cells in each drop of blood than men. Yes, you read that correctly: Take one drop of male blood and one drop of female blood and you'll find *a million more* red blood cells in the man's. A man's blood also coagulates faster than a woman's.

We come from a long line of hunter-gatherers, and some of these sex differences must have come about because in all hunter-gatherer societies on record (except for one: the Agta of the Philippines), there is a division of labor by sex. Men did the hunting, women did the gathering.

Some of the earliest sex-difference studies showed that men are better at hitting targets with projectiles than women. And in all the research since then, this has been one of the most consistent findings.

Okay, some researchers said, it makes sense that men would be superior at hunting tasks — superiorities like being able to hit a target with a projectile. Fine, they said. Good. But wouldn't gatherers *also* develop some superiorities? Like being able to locate berry bushes and tuber patches and nut trees?

So the researchers set up some experiments to find out. In one experiment, a table was piled with objects. A comb, a dishrag, a hammer, a typewriter, a book, etc. — one big jumbled pile of different objects. A man or woman was brought into the room and told to look at the pile for some specified length of time, say, two minutes. Then the man or woman was escorted out of the room.

Then the researchers would either remove an object or move it to a different location in the pile.

The subjects were brought back in and asked if the pile looked any different. Sure enough, the women were better able to detect a change in location than the men. Women have a superior ability to remember the locations of objects.

In fact, women are better at almost all forms of perception: better at hearing small changes in tone of voice and volume, a better perception of high sound frequencies, a better ability to distinguish between different tastes, more nerve endings in their skin (and therefore a greater sensitivity to touch), are better at seeing in the dark, see more red hues than men, and have better peripheral vision (because they have more receptor cones and rods in the retina).

Men have better depth perception and can see better in bright light. The only auditory superiority men have is in distinguishing animal sounds.

A woman's chances are one in *fifty thousand* of being color blind; a man has a chance of one in twenty-five.

Estrogen activates the olfactory receptors, and since women have far more estrogen than men, women's sense of smell is better. Women can detect the scent of musk better than any other odor.

Her estrogen levels vary over the course of a month, and during ovulation, when her estrogen level peaks, she can detect the scent of musk 100 to 1000 times more keenly than during menstruation.

Women *notice* more. In one experiment, subjects were told the researchers weren't ready to start the experiment yet and asked each subject (one at a time) to wait in a small room for two minutes.

Afterward, the subjects were asked what they could recall from the room they were in. That was the whole experiment.

The women remembered an incredible amount of detail. They would say things like, "There was a shelf against the wall crowded with things. There was an open pack of Wrigley's gum, a book on Greek history, a black sock, a worn out tan colored knapsack, etc." Rich detail.

When they asked the men the same question, they apparently hadn't paid much attention: "It seems to me there was a shelf in there with some stuff on it. There was a pack of gum...some clothes or something..."

Klassy (my wife) used to tease me about not noticing things, so I was determined to pay attention. One day, feeling victorious, I said, "Hey! You moved that picture. It used to be over here."

"You're right," she said, "I did move the picture...three *months* ago!"

Men spend more time in shallow sleep as they get older, but aging doesn't affect women's sleep as much.

There is an enzyme in the stomach that breaks down alcohol before it reaches the bloodstream. The enzymes in women's stomachs break down *less than one fourth* as much alcohol as the enzymes in men's stomachs, allowing more alcohol to enter her bloodstream.

Migraines affect four times as many women as men. Women suffer from more aches and pains in general than men. Women feel some sort of discomfort 43% of the time, men 28% of the time. But men find it twice as difficult to tolerate the same amount of chronic pain a woman can tolerate.

Most men put their pants on left leg first; women usually put their pants on right leg first.

According to Dr. Brian Sietsema, the Pronunciation Editor of Merriam-Webster, men and women pronounce the TH sound (as in the word "think") differently. "Men pronounce it with the tongue slightly *behind* the upper teeth," he says, "and women with the tongue *between* the teeth."

Men tend to call each other by a word other than the person's name: dude, man, etc., and women tend to use the person's name.

Women have better coordination in their fingers. You can tell a woman's handwriting from a man's because hers shows more control.

Again, there are variations, but in general each of these differences are likely to be true between you and your mate. Likely. Not absolutely.

A man is less willing to sit and think than a woman. In a study from the University of Virginia and Harvard University, the researchers were trying to find out how easy it was for people to entertain themselves. With so many forms of entertainment available, they wondered how good people are at amusing themselves nowadays. So they sat the participants in a room by themselves with no distractions for 6 to 15 minutes (they did 11 versions of this experiment). Here's where it gets interesting.

They wired up the participants so they could give themselves a painful electric shock if they wanted to. They were allowed to try it before the experiment began, so they knew how it felt. But even though it was painful, and even though before the experiment, they said they would rather pay money than experience that shock, 67% of the men shocked themselves during the experiment. Only 25% of the women did.

In other words, most men disliked sitting and thinking so much that they'd rather feel a painful electric shock! Some women too. But the difference is pretty big. Out of every dozen women, only three shocked themselves. But out of every dozen men, *eight* shocked themselves.

Here's another one: During an argument between husband and wife, her blood pressure rises, on average, 6%, whereas his rises 14%. His blood pressure rises *more than twice* what hers does. Logically, you'd think it'd be just the opposite since she is potentially in more physical danger.

But the differences go beyond logic. They are differences built into our brains and bodies, and the only criteria for the choosing was *survival*. If a trait survived and the carrier of that gene had offspring, that particular pattern of DNA went on to have more offspring. If it didn't have any offspring, it didn't pass its genes to us.

Apparently there was some advantage to having calm women and reactive men. Although those traits may no longer be an advantage, we're stuck with the biology we've got.

Men die sooner or more often in 57 of the 64 major causes of death. In fact, says, Deborah Wingard, an epidemiologist at the University of California, San Diego, "If you look at the top ten or twelve causes of death, every single one kills more men."

Dangerous Denial

Denying the biological differences between men and women can be dangerous. There's a drug prescribed for high blood pressure called Propanolol. It has been discovered that Propanolol is broken down far more slowly in women's bodies than men's. Doctors had to lower the dosage for women so they weren't continually overdosed.

A hormone called DHEAS reduces the risk of heart disease in men and contributes to their longevity. But this hormone has the opposite effect on women (it *increases* their risk of heart disease).

Twice as many women experience depression than men, and women take 83% of all antidepressants. But the studies on these drugs were done on men. Naturally, if the differences in the sexes are only caused by socialization, then a drug that works for men should work just as well for women. Of course. That's the politically correct view. But Jean Hamilton, M.D., a researcher from Duke University, found that women's menstrual cycles affected their reaction to psychotropic drugs (like antidepressants), in some cases causing serious trouble.

For years, doctors told us the warning signs of a heart attack: A dull pain in the center of the chest and/or pain down the left arm. Recent research has found, however, that those are men's symptoms. Women often experience pain in the back, neck or jaw, or they have nausea, or light-headedness, and often no chest pain. I wonder how many women have had heart attacks because they ignored these symptoms?

The sexes are not the same. They react to drugs differently. They show different symptoms. It is not simply a matter of opinion. It is not just a theoretical issue. It is not merely an interesting subject of intellectual debate. An ignorance of the differences can cause death.

Fat Differences

The differences go on and on. And all were created by the hormone that dominated in the womb: estrogen or testosterone.

In women, there are fibers that hold skin to the muscles in parallel cords. This causes the fat in between to bulge, producing what's called *cellulite*. In men, the fat is held in place by a dense mesh of fibers, making cellulite much less likely.

Men tend to store body fat around their waist, which produces more cholesterol and triglycerides than storing it in the butt and thighs, where women tend to store most of their fat.

One of the reasons men are more susceptible to atherosclerosis and heart disease is the different way they store fat. Fat on the waist is easier to burn. Fat on thighs is more resistant. It's safety fat. Women with this fat had more babies survive in times of scarcity. Female mammals (including humans) are able to withstand food deprivation for a longer period of time before dying than their male counterparts.

A woman's muscles are less striated, making them weaker but more efficient at burning blood sugar. A man has one and a half times as much muscle and bone as a woman, and half as much fat.

Estrogen affects how much fat a person *wants* to eat. Humans and other animals have a substance called galanin in their bloodstreams. Galanin produces a desire to eat fat specifically, and makes the fat consumed more likely to be converted to body fat.

Sarah Lebowitz, in her experiments at Rockefeller University, found that if you give a cow an extra shot of galanin, the cow eats more fat.

Lebowitz has also found a molecule — called M40 — that blocks the production of galanin. When she administered M40 to animals, they had no taste for fat at all. They ate protein and carbohydrates, but showed no interest in eating fat.

Lebowitz discovered two things that stimulate the human body to produce more galanin. One is the by-products of burning body fat. This makes sense: Your body notices you've burned off some fat, and it stimulates your appetite for fat so you can replace what you've burned.

The other thing that stimulates the production of galanin is estrogen.

Women have more estrogen and more body fat. This is genetic; not subject to change by socialization. We may or may not like it. DNA doesn't care about our personal, social or political ideals.

A woman has more fat covering her entire body, giving her greater protection against the cold and more buoyancy in the water.

Do you remember the couple who got lost in a snowstorm, took the wrong road and ran out of gas? They sat in their car for a day or so and then realized they better find help — no one had driven by in two days.

They got out and started walking. They had no food. They had their infant with them.

Finally, they realized they were headed in the wrong direction. They decided that the mother and baby should hole themselves up in a tiny cave and the husband should go back the way they came and find help.

He walked for *days* and finally found a road and got help. They found his wife and child in good health.

Days without food, in freezing weather, and they were fine. The baby was as healthy as could be. Through lactation, using the extra fat on the mother's body, the baby survived.

Our ancestors went through similar adverse conditions many times: Famines, terrible weather, exposure, epidemics, bad water, you name it. Lots of them didn't survive. Those whose children survived were our ancestors. Our bodies are the design that can survive extreme conditions.

Some important features that helped those offspring (our ancestors) survive were certain differences between males and females. And those differences are deep and extensive.

At one time differences between the sexes were used to prove that "men are the superior sex." Because of this, during the women's movement it became unfashionable and even rude to discover or point out gender differences.

But it is impossible to say which sex is superior by studying the differences. Each sex has its own strengths and weaknesses. Neither is "superior." Being physically bigger is usually better in a wrestling match, but what good does it do if the task is nursing a child or locating a berry bush? Or creating a satisfying relationship with another human being? Or swimming the English Channel?

In 1926 Gertrude Ederle attempted to swim the English Channel, a feat no woman had ever attempted. A writer for a London newspaper was so sure she wouldn't make it, he wrote an editorial *before she started* saying that her failure to cross the channel only showed that women should not attempt to enter competitive athletics because they were so obviously physically inferior.

But Gertrude Ederle not only made it across the Channel, she broke the existing men's record by two hours! The world record is *still* held by a woman. It is hard for men to compete — women have superior biology for the task.

The London paper went to press before the editorial could be withdrawn, and the editor had to eat the crow he completely deserved.

Let's stop thinking in terms of a "superior" sex. It's like asking, "Which is superior, a sponge or a knife?" It depends entirely what you are trying to do.

Let's focus instead on what we can do together. We can share our strengths with each other and *as a unit* become greater than the sum of our parts.

WOMEN ARE
THE STRONGER SEX

So far I've talked about some of the physical differences between the sexes, because I wanted to give you an idea of how pervasive the differences are. We're not talking about a few trivial differences in genital structure. Women and men are different to the bone (literally). When you realize that even our red-blood count is different, it becomes easier to accept that some of the more subtle differences might also be built-in and less subject to change than you thought.

Let's look at one of the more subtle differences now — a difference that can significantly affect your relationship with your mate.

When a man and a woman talk, he will tend to interrupt her more than she will interrupt him.

There's probably not a woman alive who would be surprised by that fact. Something you read in most books on human relations is that a good general policy when interacting with people is to try not to interrupt them. Women are better at it than men.

Anat Rafaeli, of the Hebrew University of Jerusalem, sent teams of observers to 600 convenience stores and observed over 11,000 interactions between the clerk and a customer. Female clerks smiled more, made more eye contact, and thanked people more than male clerks. In other words, the women practiced better human relations.

Men and women, ranging in age from 17 to 80, were given a questionnaire that asked each respondent what kinds of things he or she talked about when talking to someone of their same sex. Women spend more time than men talking about relationships and emotional issues. So not only are women generally *better* at human relations, they are more *interested* in relationships.

Women have a biological advantage when it comes to relationships. To be good at relating, you would need the ability to perceive well. If you can see and hear well, you are better equipped to perceive the feelings of other people. This would help you relate to them. And as I pointed out in the previous section, women visually notice more detail and hear changes in tone better than men.

To be good at relating, another extremely useful strength would be the ability to perceive the feelings of others and to articulate your own feelings. And here again, women have a genetic advantage. Let's take a look at some of the research.

Using what is called the PONS test (the Profile of Nonverbal Sensitivity test), Robert Rosenthal and his colleagues at Harvard University found women to be consistently better at knowing what emotional situation they're seeing when they view the short film clips that make up the test.

In the 220 two-second film clips, the experimental subjects see a person's face only, body only, or face and body both. The woman is saying something, but the actual *content* of what she's saying has been obliterated, while still retaining the tone of her voice and the rhythm of her speech.

After observing each film clip, the viewers are shown two written descriptions of the situation. The subject is asked to choose which description fits the segment they observed. Women did better than men.

There were *some* men who scored as well as the *average* woman. These were usually men working in theater or arts where selection for nonverbal sensitivity plays an important role. But these exceptional men only did as well as the *average* woman.

At the time of the original experiment, the results were explained with the Socialization Theory: "Women are nonverbally more sensitive than men because of their upbringing." But recent research shows the experiment in a whole new light.

Cecil Naylor of the Bowman-Gray School of Medicine gave experimental subjects a task, and then, using a radioactive tracer, watched to see what parts of the subject's brain was active during that task. For example, in one task the subject listened to words, one after the other, and when he or she heard a word that was four letters long, they raised a finger. During this task, the women's brains were active all over, but the men's brain activity was compartmentalized.

Another task was singing *Row Row Row Your Boat*. Places on both sides of women's brains showed activity, but for men, only one side of the brain was active.

During an oral spelling test, women and men did equally well. But during the test, the men's brains showed an intense activity in two discrete areas: Wernicke's area (in the left temporal lobe), and Broca's area (in the left frontal lobe). Wernicke's is known to play an important role in language comprehension and language creation. This is the place where language is assembled for outgo and understood when it is inflowed. And Broca's area seems to play a part in controlling the mouth, tongue, face, jaw and throat.

In women, Naylor found blood flowed heavy, not only to those two areas (Wernicke's and Broca's in the left hemisphere), but also to the right hemisphere, in the same spot as Wernicke's but on the opposite side, an area known to be involved in a particular aspect of language: emotional expression and emotional comprehension.

In men, when the communication is ready to be spoken, only Broca's area is active. In women, says Naylor, "almost every area of the cortex, left and right hemisphere, has some unique relationship with Broca's during the task, as if there were many independent things going on between Broca's and lots of different regions."

Women have more going on in their brains when communicating. They use more of their brains when talking to another person than men do. And they have a richer experience of the *emotional* reality of the relationship. And emotion is the foundation of closeness, bonding, affection, and love in relationships.

Women are the big, strong sex when it comes to relationships.

These findings might also help explain "women's intuition." Since she is perceiving more of what's going on — nonverbal communication, small changes in skin color, facial expressions, body movements, and tone of voice — and her brain is more *active*, she's perceiving things outside the man's range of perception. It would look to a man as though she were psychic.

INSIDE THE BRAIN

There are parts of the corpus callosum (the bundle of nerve fibers that connect the right and left hemispheres of the brain) that are up to 23% wider in women than in men. There are also thicker connections between the two hemispheres in other parts of women's brains. This is especially significant because men's brains are bigger than women's. Women have more gray matter too (the cells that actually perform thinking).

We're looking at a *structural* difference in the brains of women and men, a difference that helps explain some common complaints of married couples, like why women seem to be more proficient at communicating their feelings.

Emotions are processed in the right hemisphere and language is in the left hemisphere (I'll explain that in more detail in a moment). More connections between hemispheres make it easier for women to *articulate* what they feel.

To add to men's handicap in relating, their brains are more neatly compartmentalized than women's. If you give a man an abstract problem to work on, he will tend to use the right side of his brain. A woman, on the other hand, will use both sides.

Even in tests on children, it has been found that while a boy is engaged in some abstract problem (like trying to figure out what three dimensional objects can be made out of a flat piece of paper) the electrical activity of his brain is concentrated in his right hemisphere. In girls, again, the activity is in both hemispheres.

When the abstract problem was shown only to their left eye, the boys performed better on the test than when they saw it with both eyes (the left eye goes to the right hemisphere of the brain).

Girls got the same score with either eye.

Were boys *taught* to use only one side of their brains? Were girls *taught* to use both sides? For the hardcore Strictly-Socialization Theorists, they must have been.

But the evidence against that conclusion keeps mounting. For example, there is a malfunction of hormone production called Turner's syndrome that gives us a unique look at the effect of hormones on the brain. Turner's syndrome happens when girls are missing an X chromosome. In normal girls, their ovaries produce a small amount of male hormone, but girls with Turner's syndrome have no ovaries and no testicles, so they have *no testosterone whatsoever.* When these girls are given the same brain-activity tests mentioned above, they show an even *greater* degree of uncompartmentalized electrical brain activity and blood flow (more than normal girls).

Studies of men who were underexposed to male hormones in the womb (less than normal males) show brain activity more like a woman's (less compartmentalized).

While the brain is developing in the womb, sex hormones create what are called their "organizational effects" (the hormones permanently alter brain function). Then at puberty, hormones create their "activational effects" (effecting ongoing processes like aggressiveness, menstruation, voice deepening, muscle growth, hair growth, sex organ development, etc.).

Doreen Kimura (professor of psychology, and the chief researcher at the University of Western Ontario) tested women seven to ten days before the onset of menstruation (when they had high levels of estrogen and progesterone), and also three to five days *after* menstruation, when their hormone levels were low. She tested half the women in the first phase and the other half in the second phase so the results wouldn't be influenced by learning.

The women performed better at articulation, manual dexterity and verbal fluency when estrogen and progesterone were high. And they scored better on spatial tests in the low phase.

This shows, not a difference in the *sexes*, but a difference in *hormones*. It just happens that this usually translates into a difference in the sexes.

Kimura and her colleagues also found that the parts of the brain related to grammar, spelling and writing are located close together in women's brains, but are spread out in men (some in the front of the brain, the rest in the back of the brain). This makes a difference because the closer brain parts are to each other, the faster and more efficient their interactions are.

The Two Hemispheres

Your brain is divided into two halves, and each half specializes. The right hemisphere handles spatial orientation and music, recognizes faces, and deals with emotions. The left handles language. Most people have heard this much. But here's something most people don't know: This information came mainly from studies of war injuries. The problem is that it was all done on *men*. It was simply *assumed* that a brain is a brain is a brain, whether it is a man's or a woman's.

Men with injuries to their left hemisphere are unable to speak, but they can sing. Men with injuries to their right hemisphere are unable to recognize the faces of their own wife and children. They get lost in their own house, unable to find their way around. They can talk, but it's an eerie monotone, completely devoid of emotion.

But that only applies to *men*.

At his research center in Maryland, psychologist Herbert Landsel studied epileptics who had part of their brain removed. He found that the same surgeries don't impair women as much as men. Even with the removal of significant portions of their right hemisphere, women can still get around the house and recognize faces.

With the same surgery to the left hemisphere, men are three times more likely to suffer a language problem as women.

Research at the University Hospital in Western Ontario found the same thing with brain damage from strokes and tumors: Women don't lose as many abilities from the loss of the same brain area. Both men and women suffer the loss of some ability from brain damage, but the loss shows up differently.

The brains of men and women are organized differently in a definite, measurable way.

A woman's score on vocabulary tests goes down whether her brain injury is in the left or right hemisphere. But a man's vocabulary score is *only* affected by an injury to the left hemisphere.

Experiment: Hook up electrodes to monitor brain activity, and then temporarily put a person's left hemisphere to sleep. Then ask the person a logic question — the kind of question that requires significant language processing to solve.

When researchers do this experiment, here's what they see: If the person is a man, he'll have very little brain activity in his right hemisphere (the only side of his brain that's awake), and he won't be able to come up with an answer. If the person is a woman, she will have significant activity in her right hemisphere and she *will* come up with an answer.

Men favor their right ear when listening, women listen equally with both ears.

A woman once told me (talking about men's deficits in relationship skills), "Men don't try hard enough. They just need to try harder." Yeah, that must be it. All men are lazy.

I don't think so. We'll have to come up with a better explanation than that. The truth is, there is a significant amount of evidence that a woman's brain is organized differently than a man's, and that this different organization has an impact.

Sandra Witelson (neuropsychologist) showed emotionally-charged photographs to men and women. She showed the photographs to either the left visual field (connected to the right hemisphere) or the right visual field (connected to the left hemisphere).

Women recognized the emotional content of the pictures no matter what visual field they saw it with. But men (as you might now be able to predict) only recognized the emotional content when the picture was shown to the left visual field.

According to marketing research at the University of Chicago, women are more comprehensive when they evaluate a product. They take more factors into consideration when making a decision.

Advertisers have learned that if you want an ad to appeal to women, you have to give them *several* selling points, but if you want it to appeal to men, you should focus on only *one* good reason why the thing is worth buying.

We've seen that the brains of men and women are differently organized with regard to language and expressing feelings. But this doesn't prove anything. Maybe it's possible that socialization could affect the way the brain grows. And socialization for sure can affect skills like language ability. So maybe adult brains are organized differently, but that doesn't prove that those differences are determined by biology. So far, it might all be explained well enough by socialization.

Let's look a little earlier, then, to a time before socialization has gotten such a strong foothold.

INTEREST: HOW THE SEXES DIFFER

Researchers have found the following: Infant girls are more sensitive to touch than infant boys; girls have a better sense of smell, smile more, are more patient and less easily annoyed than boys; girls begin speaking earlier than boys, enunciate more clearly, and develop a larger vocabulary.

Language problems are much more common in boys than in girls. Boys who stutter outnumber girls who stutter five to one. Autism occurs in four times more boys than girls. Boys with aphasia (an extreme difficulty learning to talk) outnumber girls five to one. Over 75% of those with reading difficulties are boys.

Four times more boys are emotionally disturbed than girls.

Witelson did an experiment on two hundred normal boys and girls between the ages of six and fourteen. Each child was blindfolded, and an object was placed in each hand. Then the researchers took the objects out of the child's hands and put them in a pile of similar objects, and took the blindfolds off.

Asked to find the two objects they were just holding, the girls had no trouble finding the correct objects. The boys, however, were better at correctly identifying the object that had been in their left hand than they were at finding the objects in their right hand. Signals from the left hand go to the right hemisphere which is known to specialize (in males) in spatial information (like transferring physical sensations into visual information).

There are several possible explanations for the results of this experiment. It could be that girls' brains aren't as compartmentalized as boys', so they can process spatial information with either hemisphere. Or maybe the information travels between hemispheres more readily in girls. Or perhaps the girls don't process kinesthetic information in the same way the boys do. Maybe a combination of these.

Any way you look at it, the experiment shows a difference in the way these children processed the information. Even at a young age boys and girls are using their brains in different ways.

Experiments have shown that parents treat different sexed children differently. Maybe it is the parents' response to their children's interests.

These differences between the sexes are caused by the different levels of hormones each sex produces. As a fetus and in adulthood, males pro-duce more testosterone. Females produce more estrogen. As a fetus, this causes the brain to change, and as adults, it keeps certain differences intact.

Beginning in the 1940's and extending to the 1960's, millions of women were given diethylstil-bestrol (DES) to prevent miscarriages. DES is an artificial estrogen. Doctors stopped prescribing it when they found the drug had serious side effects.

Many studies have been done on the children who were exposed to DES in the womb. One of the things they found is that children — male or female — who had been exposed to extra estrogen in the womb were more group-oriented and more interested in communication and relationships than normal children of the same sex and age.

What About Interest?

The differences between women and men start in the womb and are produced by hormones. After children are born, masculine or feminine behavior is also affected by the child's parents' expectations and the role models they're exposed to. But as we've seen, the differences were there to start with, and there are some differences that cannot be eliminated, no matter how children are raised.

A friend of mine told me the following story: Her son was playing his new Nintendo game when her daughter came by and asked if she could play. He said, "You wouldn't want to play it. It's about war."

The daughter went to Mom and complained. Mom, of course, was outraged (as any politically correct woman would be), so she marched into the living room and scolded her son and said, "Girls should be able to play war games if they want to."

At this point in the story, I asked her, "Did she want to?"

The woman said, "Yes." But then she said, "Well, for a short time, and then she went in the other room to play with her jewelry. She doesn't actually like to play the game."

This kind of thing is going on all over the country. It happened to me when I was a kid, too. Well-meaning parents are trying to keep their children from sexual discrimination — either as the discriminatee or the discriminator. And that's wonderful. The thing to watch out for is blinding children to reality. It doesn't matter how good the doctrine is, it's always better to see reality than to miss reality because you can't perceive outside the limits of your doctrine. And that's exactly what's happening.

Women and men all over this country are running into difficulties in their relationships because they have been given false data: Namely, that there are no intrinsic differences between the sexes, and if there *are* any differences, they are learned and can be unlearned. It isn't true. And when you try to make something go right using faulty information as your guiding light, you're bound to run aground...and in this case, you're likely to be mystified about why it seems so difficult to understand your mate. It's like someone built a lighthouse on the wrong part of the coast. When you try to steer your ship by it, you end up on the rocks.

Andro-genital syndrome (AGS) is a condition caused by too many androgens (male hormones) before or shortly after a girl is born. The girls' genitals are partially masculinized, but this is often corrected with surgery. The changes to the girls' brains, however, cannot be altered by surgery or any other procedure. They show no interest in playing with dolls as children. But their normal sisters (who do not have AGS), raised in the same socializing environment, *are* interested in playing with dolls.

An interest in dolls, and if we can extend that into an interest in relationships, or at least an interest in motherhood, is not lain on from outside. It comes from within, and apparently *cannot* be laid on from outside.

You can affect, through socialization, the *behavior* of playing with dolls, but you cannot create *interest* in it through socialization. The interest is either there or it isn't. Ask any parent.

There are differences between the sexes in animals, of course, and they are also caused by hormones. Two Oxford anatomists — Pauline Field and Jefferey Raisman — decided to see if there were brain structure differences between male and female rats. There are. Female rats have more synapses connecting two parts of their hypo-thalamus than male rats do, the right hemisphere of a male rat's brain is measurably thicker than a female's, and the female's left hemisphere is thicker than the male's.

When they deprive a developing male rat of male hormones, his brain ends up looking like a female rat's brain.

Give a normal female rat a shot of testosterone, and she will start marking her territory with urine (something only males normally do). The same experiment done on dogs gets the same result. Testosterone-injected female dogs even lift one leg to pee.

Rats injected with estrogen are less nervous and less likely to engage in conflict with other rats. Among mammals, birds, lizards, and even fish, when you inject the animal with estrogen, it becomes less aggressive. This holds true whether the animal is male or female.

Female rats with pups lick them and keep them clean, catch them when they wander away and bring them back to the nest, defend the pups against attack by other animals, and of course, nurse the pups. Virgin female rats do none of these things.

But when scientists give virgin female rats a shot of estrogen and progesterone, the virgins begin to take care of any pups in their vicinity in the same way as mother rats (except for the nursing).

Here's an interesting experiment. Two researchers (Heidi Swanson and Richard Schuster) gave pairs of rats a task that required them to cooperate with each other. If they were able to cooperate and accomplish the task, they were rewarded with sugar water. Rats love sugar water.

They tested four kinds of pairs: pairs of females, pairs of males, pairs of castrated males, and pairs of castrated males who were given testosterone supplements.

The females cooperated and accomplished the task easily. So did the castrated males. The normal males and the castrates with the testosterone supplements learned more slowly, and some were unable to cooperate at all. They were too busy trying to dominate each other.

Our Closest Relatives

Chimpanzees are our closest genetic relatives. As a matter of fact, judging by the amount of DNA that matches exactly, chimpanzees are more closely related to humans than they are to their next-nearest relative, gorillas.

In the Arnhem colony (of chimpanzees) in the Netherlands, chimps have been observed for many years. The males often fight. Every female of that colony has been observed playing a peacekeeping role between males. The females will get two males who are angrily ignoring each other to interact peacefully again. They are facilitating relationships. When fights break out and the males begin arming themselves with rocks (which they throw with a fair amount of accuracy and damage), the females gently pry open their fingers and remove the rocks. When a male grabs another rock, the female gently but firmly takes it from his hand again.

All over the world chimps have been observed. Adult males spend most of their time alone, and females spend most of their time in the company of others. Females seem more interested in relationships than males do.

Facing the Facts

Whether we look at behavior or brain structure of adult or young human beings, or we look at animals, the evidence points to a difference between males and females; a biological, genetic difference.

It is time to face the facts: Women are better at communicating than men, and more interested in doing so. It is inborn. Women are genetically superior communicators. Therefore, women are more competent at relating.

When a woman asks her mate to open a jar, she is acknowledging one of the man's superiorities — in this case, he has more muscles in his arms and hands than she does.

Men should understand that when he has any problem with a relationship, he ought to ask his mate to help him "open the jar." Women are better at dealing with relation-ships, communication, and emotions — very real and important parts of every man's life.

And if a woman expects her mate to handle relationship issues as well as *she* can, isn't it like a man asking a woman to open her own jars? What would you think about a man who insisted his wife open her "fair share" of jars? Yet this is what many women do. "Why" many women ask, "do I always have to be responsible for making sure we stay in good communication?" Maybe it's because if you waited for him to even *notice* your relationship had a problem, it would be too late to do anything to save it!

We've talked about one important difference between men and women — where their interests lie. In the next chapter, we'll look at another big one.

THE AGGRESSIVE SEX

In every culture on this planet, boys are more aggressive than girls. That is the conclusion of researchers Eleanor Maccoby and Carol Jacklin.

In a study of elementary and junior high school classes, boys were found to be eight times more likely to call out answers than girls. In a three-year study, "Sexism in the Schoolroom of the 80's," it was found that boys participate and were called on in class more than girls — significantly more — and that *the teachers didn't realize it.*

Teachers were shown a film of a classroom discussion. When it was over, they were asked who was talking more. Most of the teachers said the girls were. Then they went back through carefully coding and counting who was talking and they discovered that the boys were out-talking the girls at a ratio of three to one.

Boys get more attention in grade school. Maybe this explains why they do better on tests in high school. Why do they get more attention? Because they're more aggressive — calling out answers, piping up with questions, etc.

I'm using the term "aggressive" in the scientific sense. In everyday talk, we usually say someone is aggressive if they are hostile, selfish or picking a fight. But anything someone does that isn't passive is aggressive. Saying "I love you" to someone is aggressive in the scientific sense. It is reaching, acting, approaching, initiating — trying to cause an effect. Interrupting someone who is talking is an aggressive act of communication.

The opposite of aggression is being passive, receptive or responsive. A boy who has a crush on a girl is being aggressive if he asks her out on a date. He is being passive if he only fantasizes about it or tries to look attractive in the hopes she'll ask *him* out.

Trini Johannesen, a teacher in Stockbridge, Michigan and vice president of the Michigan Education Association, took the advice of researchers and filmed her own classroom to be able to observe dispassionately. Johannesen noticed girls take more time to think through their answers. Boys tended to simply shout out and appeared less concerned whether their answer was right. She noticed some girls were having similar difficulties with classroom material as some boys, but the boys received more help because they were more noticeable. Says Johannesen, "The girls were simply less overt."

Psychology professor Aletha Houston (University of Kansas in Lawrence) conducted experiments at several preschools and found girls more likely to do activities that were supervised by an adult. Boys were more likely to play independently.

Studies of young children show boys like hostile humor more than girls. Boys are more likely than girls to find aggressive cartoons funnier.

Boys tend to initiate more aggression when playing. Part of the way aggression shows itself, and part of the *cause* of aggression is *competition*.

There is a strong element of competition among men. We are, after all, larger than women, an indication that at some time in our past, there was competition between men for mates. In any species where an individual mates with several others of the opposite sex, there is competition, and the competing sex grows larger or more beautiful than the noncompeting sex.

Genes — acting on male brains with male hormones — make males bigger, more competitive and more aggressive. Boys tease more than girls and use forbidden words more often. As adults, polls have shown men far more likely than women to favor military intervention in other countries.

Animals exposed to testosterone in utero display markedly more aggression as adults.

Girls who were exposed to male hormones in the womb were found to be "tomboys" — they liked outdoor roughhousing and were more physically active.

The parents weren't trying to teach these girls to be more active. In fact, parents concerned about their daughter's "boy-like" behavior is what brought them to the doctor. That's how most of these accidental exposures to male hormones were discovered.

At one time, male hormones were given to pregnant mothers who had toxemia. The hormones made the mothers feel better, but those who were pregnant with daughters found the girls behaved like boys: not interested in playing with dolls, more active, enjoyed roughhousing, and more aggressive.

The researcher June Reinisch found the same thing at the Kinsey Institute for Research in Sex,

Gender and Reproduction at Indiana University. The assessment of aggression was based on interviews with the girls' mothers, questionnaires given to the girls themselves, and independent ratings by the girls' teachers.

Reinisch gave multiple-choice tests to pairs of brothers and pairs of sisters (ages 6 to 18). The respondents were to answer how they would respond to different kinds of stressful situations.

On average, the males gave more aggressive and belligerent answers than the girls did. But boys who were exposed to extra male hormones in the womb were even *more* aggressive than their unexposed brothers, and the girls exposed to extra male hormones were measurably more aggressive than their unexposed sisters.

Melissa Hines at UCLA and a colleague watched CAH girls, ranging from two and a half years old to eight years old, at play. CAH is a condition that produces an excessive amount of male hormone in girls (because of a lack of two key enzymes). Sometimes they are born with a clitoris so large they are thought to be boys.

The researchers put the CAH girls in a room with toys of all kinds (kitchen supplies, books, dolls, board games, trucks, construction toys, etc.), and made careful notes of what they played with and for how long. They did the same thing with the girls' brothers and sisters for comparison.

The CAH girls played more with "masculine" toys than did their unaffected sisters. They played with the same toys as the boys did, played with them in the same ways, and spent the same amount of time playing with them, on average, as the boys.

A hormone is a powerful thing. It can not only change the way the body is built, but can also change what we're interested in.

Hines is perplexed by the findings. "Why," she asks, "would you evolve to want to play with a truck?" But perhaps it isn't a genetic predisposition to play with trucks, but to want to wield power or something more along those lines.

There is good reason to expect that at least some of the CAH girls' mothers would try to discourage "masculine" interests in their CAH daughters, or at least to not encourage it. But whether discouraged or not, the hormonally-influenced preferences persist.

Hormones affect us whether we want them to or not. We are animals, no matter how stylishly we cover ourselves with clothes and the trappings of modern civilization.

A man's beard grows faster when he is exposed to female pheromones (a molecule produced by certain glands in women).

When researchers sprayed male pheromones on half a doctor's waiting-room seats, women sat in the sprayed seats, and men did not, even though when asked, none of them smelled anything or had any inkling their behavior was being influenced by anything but their own conscious decision. Pheromones have no odor. They affect special nerve endings in the nose that send messages to certain parts of the brain.

The testosterone levels of men rise and fall, not only in regular rhythms during the day, but in seasonal rhythms too. Levels of testosterone are highest during the months of the most sunlight — in summer and early fall. And since testosterone is responsible for sex-drives, the rate of intercourse frequency peaks in the month of July, during the longest and sunniest days of the year.

Fertility rates, contraceptive sales and outbreaks of venereal disease all peak in summer and early fall.

Is it a coincidence that in a more primitive setting, our young are more likely to survive when born in the spring? Keep in mind that the infant-mortality rate of all hunter-gather societies is very high. Any adaptations that improved the rate of infant survival have been genetically bequeathed to you and me, including the seasonal rise and fall of testosterone.

Certain kinds of activities can raise a man's testosterone level: Fighting, watching violence (in movies, on television, boxing matches, football games, etc.), an intense emotional expression, winning or succeeding at something, and thinking about or engaging in sex.

Both men and women in positions of power have higher testosterone levels than people in lower ranks of a hierarchy. This is true for monkeys too. And when you give a small, weak male monkey at the bottom of the hierarchy a big dose of testosterone, he gets so aggressive, he'll fight his way to the top of the hierarchy by sheer feistiness!

Testosterone makes animals more prone to extreme forms of aggression: violence. Men have 10 to 20 times more testosterone than women. The higher the testosterone level in humans, the more prone to antisocial behavior, fighting, arrests, drug use, and divorce.

A study matching relationship histories and testosterone levels of over four thousand men showed that men with higher testosterone levels are less likely to marry and more likely to divorce.

In Europe, the re-offense rate for brutal rapists and child molesters is normally around 70 percent. But in some places they use an unusual method for handling this problem: castration. And it works extremely well. It drops the re-offense rate from 70 percent down to 3 percent! They either do the castration surgically or they use drugs that neutralize the male hormones in the blood. Both methods work equally well.

In a placebo-controlled study by the National Institute of Mental Health, researchers found that anabolic steroids (artificial male hormones) caused anger, violent feelings, sexual arousal, a higher energy level and more self-confidence.

Did you know that a whopping 90% of the children diagnosed as hyperactive are boys? Could it be because testosterone produces a high energy level and estrogen has a calming influence?

Rhesus monkeys have a nervous system similar to humans. The male monkeys play rougher and mount other monkeys more often than the females do.

Yet when pregnant Rhesus mothers are injected with male hormones, the female offspring behave like males.

Depending on *when* the hormone is injected, they display specific male behaviors. Give the shot at a certain stage in the pregnancy for example, and the female will play rough, but not mount other monkeys. Give the shot at another time, and she will mount other monkeys but not play rough.

The same has been found in experiments on rats.

Apparently, the different parts of their brains (and ours) develop at different stages in the womb, and depending on the presence or absence of male hormones, those parts of the brain form a male design or a female design.

Remember, the female design is what forms in the absence of male hormones. It is Nature's default design.

At McGill University, a researcher by the name of Michael Meaney found that one of the male hormones (dihydrotestosterone) directly activates a brain structure (the amygdala) and produces play-fighting in juvenile male rodents.

You know they can teach rats to learn a maze by giving them a reward at the end, right? Well, they've found that male rats will learn the maze even if the only reward at the end is the opportunity to fight with another male rat.

In adult male mice, the more testosterone they have, the faster they will attack a strange male in their territory. Castrate them and they become less aggressive and less territorial.

In the hypothalamus, there is a small cluster of cells called the SDN (sexually dimorphic nucleus). We know that in animals, the SDN is responsible for mating behavior, sexual response, and territorial marking. In humans, the SDN is two and a half times bigger in men than in women.

In rats, the male SDN is also bigger than in females. But give a female a prolonged dose of male hormones in the womb and her SDN grows just as big as a male's. Castrate a male just after birth and half his SDN neurons die within 24 hours.

The point is, different parts of the brain are different sizes in males and females, and these different sizes are caused by different levels of hormones while the fetus is developing. And further, these differences in brains show up as differences in *interests* and *behavior*. We may not like it, but that doesn't mean it isn't so.

Men are more aggressive than women. That's a fact. Testosterone makes men more aggressive, and estrogen makes women less aggressive.

I could go on and on. The amount of research on men's aggression is even more extensive than research on women's ability to communicate. Men are more aggressive than women.

To some people, this is a count against men. But aggression is only "bad" for certain forms of expression. And it is "good" (useful, advantageous, more effective) for others. It's safe to say the human race would not exist today without a sizable aggressive capacity.

Aggression helps get things done. Sure, a lot of what gets accomplished is destructive. But that doesn't mean *aggression* is bad. Aggression is only a power, like hydrogen. You can use hydrogen to power a hydrogen car, or you can use it to make a hydrogen bomb. The power itself is not good or bad; it depends on what you do with it.

Aggression needs to be channeled into constructive, productive, life-enhancing projects. There is plenty that needs to be done. Let's harness the power of aggression and put it to work.

WHAT DOES IT ALL MEAN?

If you want to say it with political correctness, here it is: Nature is a sexist pig. There are quite a few people, as you may have noticed, who are afraid of that fact. They don't want you or me to know about this research, and for a very good reason. This information can be used — in fact, *has* been used — to justify unkind, unfair, or intolerant treatment of one sex or the other (usually women, since men have been using the information more aggressively).

But that's not a good reason to ignore a fact. Perfectly valid and potentially useful facts are misused all the time. It isn't a comment on the danger of the facts, it's a comment on the danger of a closed mind.

A closed mind is only seeking to reinforce an already existing bias. And biases exist in the absence of facts just as readily (and maybe even more readily) than they do in the presence of facts.

Also, to say we are influenced by our biology is to imply we have less free will than we'd like to think. It may threaten women's suffrage. It might erode our concept of personal responsibility ("I couldn't help it! I was pumped up on my own testosterone at the time."). These are some of the reasons people don't want the research on the biological differences between the sexes to be well known.

A group of anthropologists met to discuss this issue. Some of them were intrigued by these findings, and some were against them for political and social reasons (as well as, I'm sure, the fact that these findings put the "socialization theory" in question, and many scholars hold that theory very dear). One of the scholars said into the microphone that these findings and the new theories coming out of them are "an attempt to justify genetically the sexist, racist, and elitist status quo in human society!" He said it will "ruin our children. It is a deterministic scam, a political plot, a vicious, pernicious disease!"

"Facts," said Aldous Huxley, "do not cease to exist because they are ignored."

Just because something is ugly and has horrible implications doesn't make it untrue. You can make whatever you want out of a fact, useful or not, but it doesn't change the fact.

The purpose of this book is not to discuss what "society" ought to do about these facts. I'm concerned with you and your relationship with your significant other, and I can tell you that an ignorance of these facts — whether deliberate or not — will make it more difficult to be happy in your relationship.

I don't believe these facts should be used to force someone into a limitation. Women may be better communicators, but some men are pretty good, and I don't think we should prevent a man from getting a job as a negotiator if he can do it well enough.

Being a cop may require a certain amount of strength and aggression, but when a woman can do the job, obviously she should be hired and paid the same as a man for the same position. That's only fair, as any rational person can see.

No pursuits ought to be denied to someone who wants to pursue it and is capable of pursuing it, for sexual, religious, racial, or any other dumb reasons.

Recognizing differences is not the same as defining differences and forcing everyone to confine themselves to the defined roles. The amount of male and female hormones in each of us varies quite a bit, and we each have different histories, so we will each have strengths and weaknesses, superiorities and inferiorities, interests and lack of interests in different things — between sexes and within each sex.

Our biology may determine how we feel and what we want, but *we* determine what we *do*. And if someone can do a job, she or he should be free to do it.

And also, we are each responsible for what we do, regardless or how we feel or what sex we are. I may be more likely than a woman to feel like hitting someone, but if either of us *actually* hit someone, the consequences should be the same.

What's In a Gene?

Genes often don't influence our behavior directly. They act through the medium of our *feelings* — what we like and what we don't like; what we're drawn to and what we have no interest in; what's comfortable and what's not. Little boys fidget because it's uncomfortable not to. It was probably adaptive at some time. Maybe it builds coordination faster to keep boys constantly moving.

Genes code for hormones and brain proteins and levels of neurotransmitters. They usually code for structure rather than specific behaviors. Most behaviors are learned in humans. In other words, genes don't program very much specific behavior in humans. They program feelings, urges, drives, likings, interests — what we will and will not enjoy. Our genes don't give us *thoughts* like "I should help my relatives," they give us *feelings*: "I *want* to help my relatives."

Some of our "masculine" or "feminine" behaviors are open to learning. But desires and preferences may not be as changeable. "Deepseated preferences cannot be argued about," said Oliver Wendell Holmes, Jr., "you cannot argue a man into liking a glass of beer." You can't convince someone to like something she or he doesn't like.

Reality First

One or more of the differences I've described in this book may not fit your particular relationship. If one doesn't, I recommend you pay more attention to the reality in front of you than to something you read.

If, however, this information hits home with you and your mate, and if you've found a trait you have resisted, fought against, or tried to make your mate get over, that's where this information becomes useful.

If you knew it wasn't your mate's fault, and the trait isn't causing you harm — it's just different and you "can't understand" it — then there is a possibility of reconciling yourselves to each other in a new, more intimate way. This information gives you a way of understanding things that seemed incomprehensible before.

I remember years ago Klassy and I got into an argument because she criticized me. At least in my mind, that's what started it. In her mind, it was probably because I did something stupid and she criticized me justifiably.

But after a lot of (sometimes heated) discussion, I realized that I was assuming she is like me. I assumed that she was feeling like I would have to feel (intense anger) before I would approach her with a criticism.

But the fact is, she lives in a different world, hormonally speaking. That's incontrovertible. When researchers hook up men and women in an argument to bio-measuring machines, they find that during conflict, men are experiencing more stress than the women are. And there is plenty of evidence to suspect that this difference is a biologically-based difference, rather than a result of socialization.

So if I assume Klassy is experiencing things the way I am, my assumption will miss the mark — it will be false — and when I take action on a false assumption, my actions are liable to be inappropriate. In this case, inappropriate actions on my part were then misunderstood by Klassy: She thought I was overreacting or I misunderstood her or something. It became confusing. We then tried to clear up the confusion, but no matter how much we restated our positions and tried to understand each other, it remained confusing because you have to back up all the way to the beginning assumption (that we are experiencing this event similarly because we are the same) in order to clear things up.

Later, when the fight was over, I just wanted to say, "Oh well, let's be friends and forget about it," and go on about our day. She doesn't let go of things so easily. This also seems to be a genetically-caused difference. Chimpanzees, who share 99.6% of our active DNA, show the same pattern: Males make up after conflicts fairly quickly. Females can hold grudges for years.

Males doing battle alongside other males of their group, defending territory and hunting co-operatively (as chimpanzees do) don't survive very well if they hold grudges, so somewhere along the line, a tendency developed in males to try to reconcile conflicts quickly.

Nowadays, it may be useful or not, I don't know. But what I do know is this: It is a lot easier to deal with Klassy when I assume she is different than when I assume she is like me. Much less of her behavior frustrates or confuses me.

Let's get off each others' backs about our differences. Let's quit trying to make each marriage partner do an equal amount of everything. "Whoever thinks marriage is a 50-50 proposition," said Franklin P. Jones, "doesn't know the half of it."

Let yourselves specialize into different divisions of labor if that's what seems natural and easy and pleasant. If you have one person who really cares about having a clean house, and whose standards are high, and the other partner doesn't care about having a clean house and whose standards are low anyway...guess who's going to end up doing more housework? If a woman was willing to let the house get as dirty as he's willing, then there wouldn't be a conflict, would there?

If he likes fixing the car and she likes doing the housework, and he likes working more hours at his job and she likes spending more time with the kids, what's wrong with that?

It's a difference in *interest*. Why are some people interested in computers and some people interested in astronomy? Who knows? But one thing is for sure: They will be happiest pursuing their interest and not trying to force themselves down a path that doesn't give them enjoyment because they have artificial standards of behavior they try to conform to.

Biological Creatures

Does this mean we're at the mercy of our biology? Yes and no. What biology is doing is affecting our *feelings*. But you can do something even when you don't feel like it, and you can feel like doing something and yet refrain from doing it. It's called self-discipline.

It's obviously a genetic compulsion to eat when we're hungry, yet people have been known to deliberately refuse to eat until they died of starvation.

But some genetic impulses are not worth resisting. And what we like to do most is one of those. Yes, you can go without food, but you still *feel* hungry. You can behave as if you like things or are interested in things you aren't, but pretending all the time is unpleasant. Not only that, in a relationship, it causes confusion and resentment. And besides, it's dishonest.

I'm taking it for granted you wouldn't do something that harmed another person. But given that qualification, why should you do something you don't like to do and keep yourself from doing something you like, when it doesn't harm anyone? That's not a prescription for happiness.

Let's take another look at the Socialization Theory and our sex differences. Maybe our differences could be a strength. Maybe it's not a bad thing at all. Maybe it's a blessing.

It's true that men could act more like women and women could act more like men. But what kind of an empty life would that be? I don't like being something I'm not. I don't like acting or pretending. It is an unsatisfying way to live. Not only that, but behaving incongruently with the way you really feel is a formula for a superficial relationship: Just be phony and act the way your lover wants you to, pretend you like things you don't, and you are sure to have a shallow, unsatisfying relationship.

But we don't have to be the same to be intimate.

Where We Go From Here

Socialization is something you've learned, and it can be changed by learning something new. Genetics is not learned, it's built in, and you have to either accept it or work around it. Our species has a genetic predisposition to male dominance of females, for example. We work around it with laws and social attitudes. Birth control is another example. The desire to mate can't be changed. It's genetic and unchangeable. But we have worked around it with contraception: The purpose of sex (from a genetic standpoint) has been circumvented.

If your partner seems unable to change some particular characteristic, it is possible, especially if it fits a sex-role stereotype, that it's genetic and unchangeable. So what are you supposed to do?

First Take the Blame Out

Men and women are not to blame for their differences. Do you blame men for being hairy? Do you blame women for being short? If you had two people, one of whom was color-blind and one who had good color discrimination, who would you ask to decorate your house? Would anyone be blamed? Mocked? Bashed? Would anyone be pushed to change?

If there are things you would like your mate to change (and there are), and you come to him or her with an attitude of blame, you create resistance, not cooperation.

If what you want your mate to change is unchangeable, the resistance turns into resentment and frustration. But the information in this book can help you take the blame out of your request, and together you can find ways of working around those characteristics if they can't be changed.

No one is at fault. It's just life. It's just what survived billions of years of evolution. No one is to blame.

I don't verbalize my feelings very easily. Given that I'm a male, the evidence suggests that this is probably because male hormones compartment- talized my brain, gave me a smaller corpus callo- sum, and made me less sensitive in the womb. Klassy used to get annoyed with me (and I was annoyed at myself) and she would say, "Why didn't you just tell me you felt that way?"

Well, I didn't really "know" I felt that way. Or, I "sort of" knew. I knew how I felt nonverbally. But it didn't show up for me as something to say. It's hard to put something in words that doesn't seem to be available in words.

I now compensate for this by taking the time to concentrate and ask myself what I feel and try to articulate it. But as long as I've been doing this, I'm not much better at it.

Klassy has a genetic strength where I have a weakness and she no longer gets annoyed with me. She helps me instead, just like I don't get annoyed at her for being unable to reach the top shelf. I help her instead.

Let's not only give up blame, but venture beyond it. Let's see what kind of relationships we can develop given our realities rather than our culture's myths and fantasies. Every step you take in this direction will make you more satisfied with each other, more comfortable and relaxed around each other, and less phony. And you'll have less futile conflict.

Take Advantage

Klassy helps me build business relationships and relationships with my family. I help her accomplish her goals. She helps me think things through. I help her stay on track. Not only have we finally stopped fighting against our differences, we're learning to capitalize on each other's strengths.

Men and women work well as a unit, like a pilot and navigator. When flying a plane, the pilot and navigator don't try to be fair. The pilot doesn't make the navigator do his "fair share" of the piloting. It's inefficient. It wouldn't work as well. Instead, they each do what they do best because when they do, each is better off as part of the team than either would be alone.

Researchers at Stanford University found that women and men have different responses to depression and that these differences may help explain why the rate of depression among women is twice that of men (and, by the way, why alcoholism in men is twice that of women).

Men try to distract themselves from their bad feelings; women tend to ponder their bad feelings. When a woman is depressed, she will tend to focus her thoughts on what is causing the depression and think about possible consequences. Men tend to use an activity that requires their attention to help them avoid thinking about the problem (or use alcohol to reduce their ability to think about anything).

You can see that neither option is the best one for everything. If the problem is small and/or can't be changed, it is better to distract yourself with a challenging or engaging, and maybe even pro-ductive task. But if the problem is big and/or *can* be changed, it is better to think it through and make some decisions.

This is just one example. We have a lot we can learn from each other. We can lean on each other and find strength.

There are genetically determined differences between all of us, even between people of the same sex. Let's develop a little more tolerance for each other. Let's learn to resist the urge to fight against those differences or try to make everyone the same and instead, let's try to discover the advantages of our differences, and in this way, help to realize and enjoy the full benefits of being human.

Note: If you'd like to absorb this material even better, I have recorded the whole thing as a podcast, which you can listen to for free on your favorite podcast platform:

https://www.adamlikhan.com/2020/10/the-differences-between-sexes-have-real.html

ABOUT THE AUTHORS

Adam Khan blogs at adamlikhan.com and hosts The Adam Bomb podcast. He's the author of the books, *Self-Help Stuff That Works*, *Principles For Personal Growth* (now being used as a textbook for a college course in San Diego), *How to Change the Way You Look at Things (in Plain English)*, *Direct Your Mind*, *Cultivating Fire: How to Keep Your Motivation White Hot*, *Antivirus For Your Mind*, and *Self-Reliance, Translated*.

Adam has been published in *Prevention Magazine*, *Cosmopolitan*, *Body Bulletin*, *Your Personal Best Newsletter*, *Wisdom*, *Think and Grow Rich Newsletter*, *the Success Strategies* newsletter, and he was a regular columnist for *At Your Best* (a Rodale Press publication) for seven years where his monthly column was voted the readers' favorite. Write to him at adamkhan@usa.com.

Klassy Evans began conducting communication seminars and workshops in the business and private sector in 1982. She is also the creator of the seminars, *The Happiness Course* and *How to Handle People Who Bring You Down*. And she is the editor of *Self-Help Stuff That Works* and *Principles For Personal Growth*. Write to her at klassy@usa.com.

APPENDIX: OTHER INTERESTING DIFFERENCES

We stopped writing this book years ago, but since publishing this book, we've continually come across more interesting differences in lots of different contexts. Here they are, in no particular order.

1. Most women have a better sense of smell than most men. And it's not because men aren't trying hard enough. They just don't have the processing power. Men don't have as many cells in their olfactory bulbs as women. And it is a significant difference. On average, a man has 9.2 million cells in their olfactory bulb (a combination of neurons and glial cells). A woman has 16.2 million on

average, according to researchers at the University of São Paulo.

2. Changes in language come primarily from females; most often from teenage girls. There are several ways this has been discovered. One of the more interesting was a study of thousands of letters written by women from 1417 until 1681. They compared these to writings by men in the same period and found that women changed the way they used language more quickly than men. They spread new linguistic trends and helped bring an end to outdated usages. In studying bilingual communities, another researcher found that young women were "more advanced in the direction of linguistic change than older people and young men."

3. The longer the race, the better women do compared to men. In the book *Born to Run*, the author, Christopher McDougall, was talking about Leadville, which is a 100 mile run that takes place at elevations of 9,200 to 12,600 feet, high in the Colorado Rockies. Ninety percent of all the women who run that race finish. Only fifty percent of the

men finish the race. If you look at shorter races, you see that in the mile race, there are no women who rank among the top fifty in the world. Sometimes there is a woman in the top twenty in the marathon. And very often in ultramarathon races (fifty to a hundred miles) women *win*. The way McDougall put it, the gap between male and female champions gets smaller as the race gets longer.

4. Women endure starvation better than men. In a fascinating book, *The Great Starvation Experiment*, Ancel Keys studied the famines that occurred during World War II. He found women were more durable than men. When Germany occupied Greece, for example, men older than twenty died at a much higher rate from starvation than women of the same age. There was a horrendous famine in the Netherlands near the end of the war. The death rate of women rose 73 percent. But for men, the rate of death rose 169 percent. He found the same in the internment camps run by the Japanese. Women have a superior biology for surviving starvation.

5. Men and women respond differently to stress. Most of us are familiar with the "fight or flight" response. Under stress, the body is flooded with the stress hormones, adrenaline and cortisol. But researchers are discovering that this well-known pattern may be a mostly male reaction. A different kind of reaction has been discovered, termed the "tend and befriend" reaction. Women often respond to stress by connecting with others rather than fighting or fleeing. For example, in one experiment, subjects put one of their hands in ice water. It's painful and it causes a rise in stress hormones. While this was happening, their brains were scanned, and a difference between the sexes was discovered. The region of the brain devoted to reading faces became *less* active in the men's brains, but became *more* active in the women's brains. Another region in women became more active too: The part of the brain that helps them understand the emotions of others. Under stress, men became physically *less* able to connect to others while women became *more* able.

6. Women have a greater tactile sensitivity than men. I mentioned this earlier in the book, but here's more detail: Scientists can measure a person's ability to detect pressure on the skin, and they can be very precise about how much pressure they are applying to the skin and how much pressure it takes until the person says, "I can feel that." Females of all ages have a greater sensitivity to touch on every part of their body than men. As I've mentioned before, the differences in the sexes often overlap. But on this measure, in some tests, there was no overlap. In other words the *most* sensitive man was less sensitive than the *least* sensitive woman.

7. Women's brains make less serotonin than men's brains. Some researchers believe this is why twice (or more) as many women suffer from depression as men.

8. Women wake up from anesthesia faster than men do. Women take, on average, seven minutes to come out of anesthesia. Men take eleven minutes.

9. According to the Society for Women's Health Research, reactions to medications

can be very different for women than men, including antibiotics and antihistamines. And they point out four drugs that were being prescribed to both men and women that have been taken off the market because the health risk to women was so much greater than to men.

10. Autoimmune diseases affect far more women than men. Seventy-five percent of people with lupus, multiple sclerosis, and rheumatoid arthritis are women.

11. Men react to some pain medications differently than women. For example, ibuprofen works better for men than women. And kappa-opiates (used for pain relief after surgery) work far better for women than men.

12. Sue Johnson says that when their relationship is in trouble, "men typically talk of feeling rejected, inadequate, and a failure; women of feeling abandoned and unconnected." Johnson created a couples therapy called Emotionally Focused Therapy, which has been shown in independent studies to

be the most effective form of couples therapy.

13. The same author, Sue Johnson, says that when she asks couples to reveal to each other their attachment fears and longings, "the female partner will probably find this task easier." Throughout her book, Johnson goes out of her way to play down differences between the sexes, sometimes explaining them as mere socialization. And still, she can't help but acknowledge important differences because it comes up again and again in her counseling sessions, and the many studies on the subject are impossible to dismiss. The reason women will probably find the task easier, Johnson says, is: "Women have been shown in many studies to retain stronger and more vivid memories of emotional events than do men. This appears to be a reflection of physiological differences in the brain, not a sign of the level of involvement in the relationship."

14. Does it seem like your mate likes the temperature of the room colder or hotter than you do? This may be a biological difference.

I just read a little article in a really great newsletter called *The Whippet*. A study on bats found that female bats stayed in the warmer valleys and the male bats tended to go to the higher, cooler mountain areas. Across the board, in both birds and mammals, females feel colder. Their core temperatures are actually not any colder, but they feel colder, and the researchers think it's an evolutionary adaptation to making sure their offspring stay warm. If the mother feels cold, she will tend to stay in warmer places. Very young animals are not very capable of staying warm.

15. I came across another one just today. It was from an interview with Stephen Kopecy, MD, a heart specialist at the Mayo Clinic. He was talking about research on using aspirin daily to prevent heart attacks and strokes. In the interview, he said, "Aspirin reduces the risk of stroke in women but not in men (first stroke). Aspirin reduces the risk of a heart attack in men, but not women."

16. In a study by several prestigious universities including Cambridge and Harvard — a

study that included over 300,000 people in 57 countries — researchers found that women are better than men at knowing what someone else is thinking and feeling. David M. Greenberg, the lead scientist of this study, said, "Our results provide some of the first evidence that the well-known phenomenon — that females are on average more empathic than males — is present in a wide range of countries across the globe. It's only by using very large data sets that we can say this with confidence."

17. Hypothyroidism is ten times more common in women than men. That's a condition where something is wrong with your thyroid gland and your body doesn't produce enough thyroid hormone. This seems un-likely to have anything to do with socializ-ation.

18. Over the counter pain relievers not only relieve some kinds of physical pain, but they can also reduce *emotional* pain. In a recent study at the University of Texas by Anita Vangelisti, however, it appears to work only

on women. For men, it made emotional pain *worse*.

♦♦❖♦♦